CARTOON FUN

Frank Rodgers

SCHOLASTIC INC.
New York Toronto London Auckland Sydney

ISBN 0-590-45035-2

12 11 10 9 8 7 6 5 4 3 2   1 2 3 4 5 6/9

Printed in the U.S.A.   08

First Scholastic printing, October 1991

CONTENTS

Cartoons have been around for a long time. As far back as the 18th century artists used cartoon drawings to make famous people (usually politicians) look funny.

Cartoonists are still doing it today. This is called political cartooning.

Strip cartoons and comic strips started in the 19th century.
In the 1930s, characters like Popeye and Superman became popular and were soon followed by hundreds of others.

The drawing of animal cartoons is more recent.
The first ones appeared in strip cartoons in American newspapers at the beginning of this century. Since then, characters like Mickey Mouse, Tom & Jerry and Snoopy have become world-famous. Maybe one of *your* creations will too one day!

If you like the idea of drawing your own cartoons, then check out the rest of this book and I'll show you, step by step, how to do it. It's easy!!

FACES

Start off by drawing *faces*.

Get used to drawing funny faces of all shapes and sizes, with all sorts of expressions, before you move on to figures. A cartoon face can be any shape, depending on the type of character you want to draw . . . but to make it easy for yourself at the beginning just use a rough oval shape like this . . .

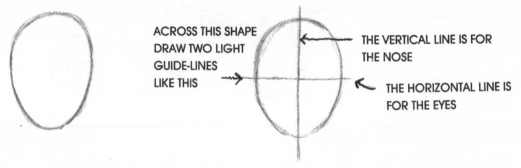

ACROSS THIS SHAPE DRAW TWO LIGHT GUIDE-LINES LIKE THIS

THE VERTICAL LINE IS FOR THE NOSE

THE HORIZONTAL LINE IS FOR THE EYES

Now you are ready to begin.

Start with the eyes. Like everything else in your cartoon you must *simplify* and *exaggerate* them. Simplify the eyes by leaving out the creases and eyelashes and exaggerate them by making them big and wide.

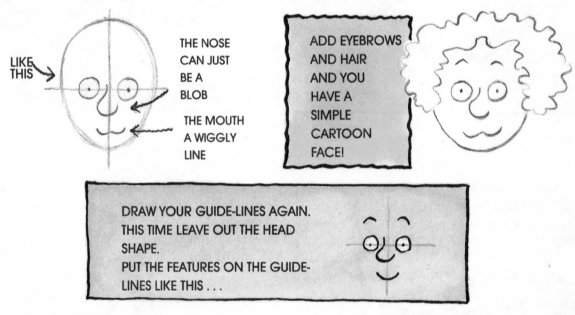

LIKE THIS →

THE NOSE CAN JUST BE A BLOB

THE MOUTH A WIGGLY LINE

ADD EYEBROWS AND HAIR AND YOU HAVE A SIMPLE CARTOON FACE!

DRAW YOUR GUIDE-LINES AGAIN. THIS TIME LEAVE OUT THE HEAD SHAPE. PUT THE FEATURES ON THE GUIDE-LINES LIKE THIS . . .

Now by drawing different face shapes round these features you can create entirely new characters.

To help you to draw a head that's looking to the side, imagine that the guide-line down the middle actually curves round the shape of the head.

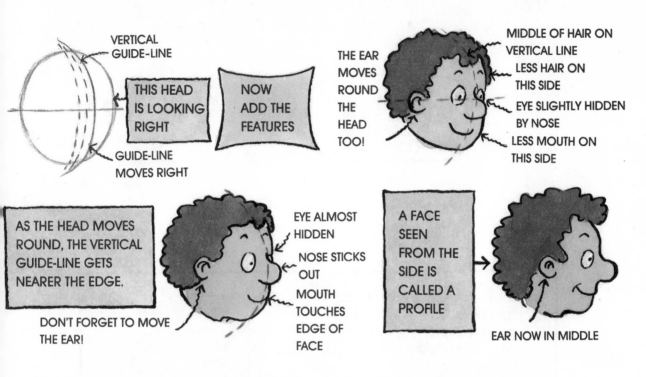

VERTICAL GUIDE-LINE

THIS HEAD IS LOOKING RIGHT

NOW ADD THE FEATURES

GUIDE-LINE MOVES RIGHT

THE EAR MOVES ROUND THE HEAD TOO!

MIDDLE OF HAIR ON VERTICAL LINE

LESS HAIR ON THIS SIDE

EYE SLIGHTLY HIDDEN BY NOSE

LESS MOUTH ON THIS SIDE

AS THE HEAD MOVES ROUND, THE VERTICAL GUIDE-LINE GETS NEARER THE EDGE.

DON'T FORGET TO MOVE THE EAR!

EYE ALMOST HIDDEN

NOSE STICKS OUT

MOUTH TOUCHES EDGE OF FACE

A FACE SEEN FROM THE SIDE IS CALLED A PROFILE

EAR NOW IN MIDDLE

Use the same technique with the horizontal guide-line and your cartoon head will look up or down.

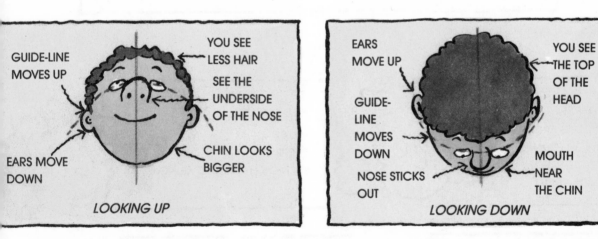

GUIDE-LINE MOVES UP

YOU SEE LESS HAIR

SEE THE UNDERSIDE OF THE NOSE

CHIN LOOKS BIGGER

EARS MOVE DOWN

LOOKING UP

EARS MOVE UP

GUIDE-LINE MOVES DOWN

NOSE STICKS OUT

YOU SEE THE TOP OF THE HEAD

MOUTH NEAR THE CHIN

LOOKING DOWN

Have a go at copying these heads, then try some of your own.

EXPRESSION

The faces at the bottom of the last page look interesting not only because they are looking around in different positions but also because each face has an *expression* on it.

An *exaggerated* expression. This is what makes a cartoon face look funny.

I SUPPOSE YOU THINK YOU'RE FUNNY.. YOU AND YOUR BLANK EXPRESSION!

Here's how to do it.

First try out the expression yourself in a mirror.

For instance, make yourself look very angry. What happens?

YOUR BROW BECOMES FURROWED,
YOUR EYEBROWS SLOPE INWARDS . . .
SO DO YOUR EYES . . .
THEY ALSO GET NARROWER,
YOUR NOSTRILS FLARE,
YOUR MOUTH TURNS DOWN
AND YOU GRIT YOUR TEETH.
NOT A PRETTY SIGHT!

Now we'll try some other expressions . . .

SURPRISE
EYEBROWS ARCHED
HIGH ON FOREHEAD,
EYES WIDE OPEN,
MOUTH A DOT

DELIGHT
SAME FACE AS
'SURPRISE'
BUT MOUTH IS NOW SMILING

DEPRESSION
EYEBROWS ANGLED UP
TOWARDS THE CENTRE
OF THE HEAD,
EYES HALF-SHUT FOLLOWING
ANGLE OF EYEBROWS,
MOUTH TURNED DOWN
AT THE CORNERS

TEARS
EYEBROWS ANGLED UP,
EYES CLOSED,
MOUTH WIDE OPEN
AND TURNED DOWN,
TEARS SPRAYING OUT

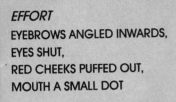

EFFORT
EYEBROWS ANGLED INWARDS,
EYES SHUT,
RED CHEEKS PUFFED OUT,
MOUTH A SMALL DOT

SNEAKINESS
EYEBROWS SLOPE INWARDS
WITH LITTLE ARCHED BITS
ON THE ENDS,
EYES NARROWED

HORROR
HAIR STANDING
ON END,
EYEBROWS ARCHED,
EYES BULGING,
MOUTH AS WIDE AS
POSSIBLE,
TONGUE AND THROAT
SHOWING

LAUGHTER
EYEBROWS ARCHED,
EYES CLOSED,
'LAUGHTER LINES' AT
CORNERS OF EYES,
MOUTH WIDE OPEN
AND TURNED UP

Here are some eyes and mouths you can use . . .

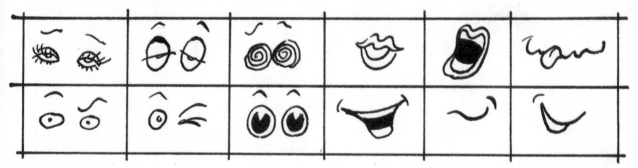

. . . to put together and create other expressions.

BODY LANGUAGE

A cartoon is much more than just a head, of course.
See how much more expressive those faces are when attached to the right kind of body. It's . . . *body language.*

ANGER
SHOULDERS HUNCHED UP, BODY LEANING FORWARD, HANDS ON HIPS, LEGS SPREAD APART

SURPRISE
ONE HAND UP TO MOUTH, THE OTHER STRETCHED OUT, BODY LEANING BACK SLIGHTLY

DELIGHT
HANDS UP, FINGERS SPREAD APART, BODY LEANING BACK, FEET OFF THE GROUND

DEPRESSION
SITTING DOWN SLUMPED FORWARD, SHOULDERS HUNCHED UP, ELBOWS ON KNEES, CHIN IN HANDS

TEARS
HANDS AT FACE
RUBBING EYES,
BODY LEANING
BACKWARDS,
ONE FOOT
BEING
STAMPED!

EFFORT
SHOULDERS
HUNCHED,
BODY BENT
FORWARD,
BOTTOM
STICKING OUT,
KNEES BENT

SNEAKINESS
SHOULDERS
HUNCHED,
ARMS UP WITH
FINGERS STRETCHED,
BODY LEANING
FORWARD,
ONE LEG LIFTED,
FEET ON TIP-TOE

HORROR
HANDS UP,
FINGERS OUT-
STRETCHED,
BODY LEANING
BACK,
LEGS WIDE APART

LAUGHTER
SIMILAR TO ANGER . . .
ONLY THIS TIME
BODY IS ANGLED
BACK,
SHOULDERS UP,
HANDS ON HIPS,
LEGS APART

As with the faces, try out the body expressions yourself in front of a mirror.
Before you do, however, it might be a good idea to read the next two pages because that's where I show you how to draw figures!

11

SIMPLE FIGURES

There are various ways of drawing *simple figures*.
One of the most common is by drawing 'stick' shapes, then 'filling out' the proper shape of the figure over them.

RUNNING *JUMPING* *WAVING* *DANCING* *THROWING*

You can try using stick figures if you want but I think they are not really helpful as it's always awkward 'filling out' the proper shape of the figure over these guide-lines.

HE DOESN'T NEED 'FILLING OUT'... JUST LOOK AT THOSE MUSCLES!

A BETTER METHOD OF DRAWING SIMPLE FIGURES IS TO USE ROUNDED 'BLOB' SHAPES, LIKE THIS

NOW DRAW THE CARTOON YOU WANT OVER THE 'BLOBS'

This method is easier than the 'stick' method because you already have a 'filled out' figure which looks a lot more like the finished shape.

RUNNING *JUMPING* *WAVING* *DANCING* *THROWING*

12

Another way is to imagine the body split up into different areas or 'bits'.

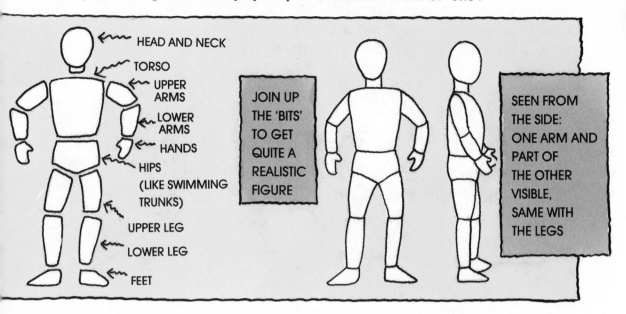

HEAD AND NECK

TORSO

UPPER ARMS

LOWER ARMS

HANDS

HIPS
(LIKE SWIMMING TRUNKS)

UPPER LEG

LOWER LEG

FEET

JOIN UP THE 'BITS' TO GET QUITE A REALISTIC FIGURE

SEEN FROM THE SIDE: ONE ARM AND PART OF THE OTHER VISIBLE, SAME WITH THE LEGS

If you think of each of these 'bits' as having a life of its own and being able to move by itself, then you'll get a better idea of how the whole body moves. For example:

HEAD LEANING LEFT

TORSO LEANING RIGHT

HIPS TILTED LEFT

LEGS BENT

YOU GET A GREAT FEELING OF 'MOVEMENT' OR 'ACTION'.
THIS FIGURE COULD BE A DANCER OR EVEN A SOCCER PLAYER.

. . . SEE WHAT I MEAN?

IMPORTANT
Remember, whatever method you use – 'stick', 'blob' or 'bits' – draw *lightly* with a pencil so you can rub out the guide-lines later!

ACTION FIGURES

When drawing *action figures* remember that the body is *flexible* and can move in almost any direction and at almost any angle.
If you don't believe me, just watch gymnasts on T.V.!

The first action figure to attempt is a running one.
If you look at someone who is running you will notice that their head and body lean forward and the arms and legs are bent. (When the *right leg* is forward the *right arm* is back.)

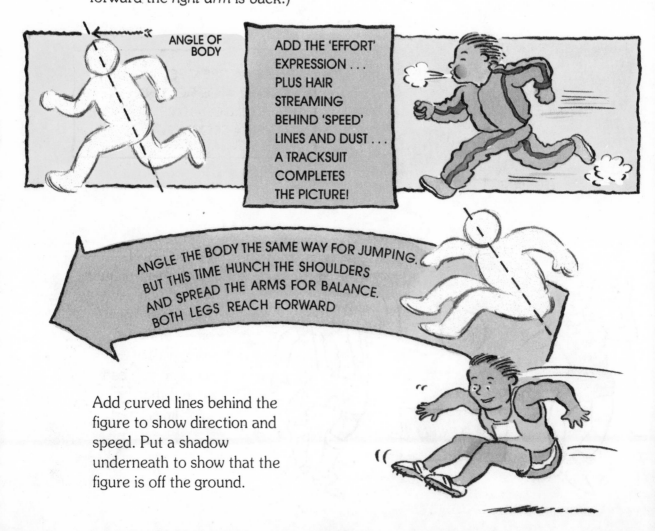

ANGLE OF BODY

ADD THE 'EFFORT' EXPRESSION . . . PLUS HAIR STREAMING BEHIND 'SPEED' LINES AND DUST . . . A TRACKSUIT COMPLETES THE PICTURE!

ANGLE THE BODY THE SAME WAY FOR JUMPING. BUT THIS TIME HUNCH THE SHOULDERS AND SPREAD THE ARMS FOR BALANCE. BOTH LEGS REACH FORWARD

Add curved lines behind the figure to show direction and speed. Put a shadow underneath to show that the figure is off the ground.

There are, of course, different ways to run and jump. Here are a few:

SPRINTING
HEAD JUTS FORWARD,
FEET LIFT HIGHER

LEAPING
ARMS ABOVE HEAD,
LEGS SLIGHTLY BENT

JOGGING
BODY DOESN'T LEAN,
HEAD HELD HIGH

DIVING
HEAD LOOKS UP, ARMS
AND LEGS STRETCHING

Every sport or game has its own kind of action and movement:

KICKING
BODY LEANS FORWARD,
HEAD LOOKS DOWN, ONE
ELBOW HIGH, OTHER LOW

HITTING
BODY LEANS TOWARDS THE SHOT,
RACKET ARM BENT, OTHER BACK
FOR BALANCE, LEGS APART

DANCING
NO SHARP ANGLES HERE,
FLOWING LINES MAKE
FIGURE LOOK GRACEFUL

PREPARING TO THROW
BODY LEANING BACK, THROWING
ARM BACK, OTHER HIGH FOR BALANCE

THROWING
LEANING FORWARD, THROWING
ARM THRUST OUT, OTHER ONE BACK

START COLLECTING
CUTTINGS FROM
NEWSPAPERS AND
MAGAZINES. PUT
THEM IN A FOLDER
OR SCRAP BOOK.
IN THIS WAY YOU
CAN BUILD UP A
'REFERENCE LIBRARY'
OF ACTION POSES.

CONTRAST

Have a look again at the two figures at the bottom of page 13, the soccer player and the dancer. These two don't look particularly funny, so here is another tip to add to *simplify* and *exaggerate* . . . it's *contrast*. (This means putting opposite things together for effect.) So how about a granny in a soccer strip and a beefy bodybuilder in a dancer's outfit?

AND IT WOULD LOOK JUST AS EFFECTIVE WITH GRANNY IN A TUTU AND MR. MUSCLES IN A SOCCER STRIP!

Here are some other contrasts:

LARGE HEAD ON A SMALL BODY

SMALL HEAD ON A LARGE BODY

CLOTHES TOO BIG

CLOTHES TOO SMALL

Or contrast one size with another.

Or exaggerate the size of a feature to make it contrast with the rest of the face.

CARTOON EFFECTS

So far, the only *cartoon effects* I have used are movement or 'speed' lines, an impact shape, dust and of course speech bubbles.

Cartoons wouldn't be cartoons without all the strange and wonderful effects that are used to make the pictures lively and funny.

Here are some of the most popular:

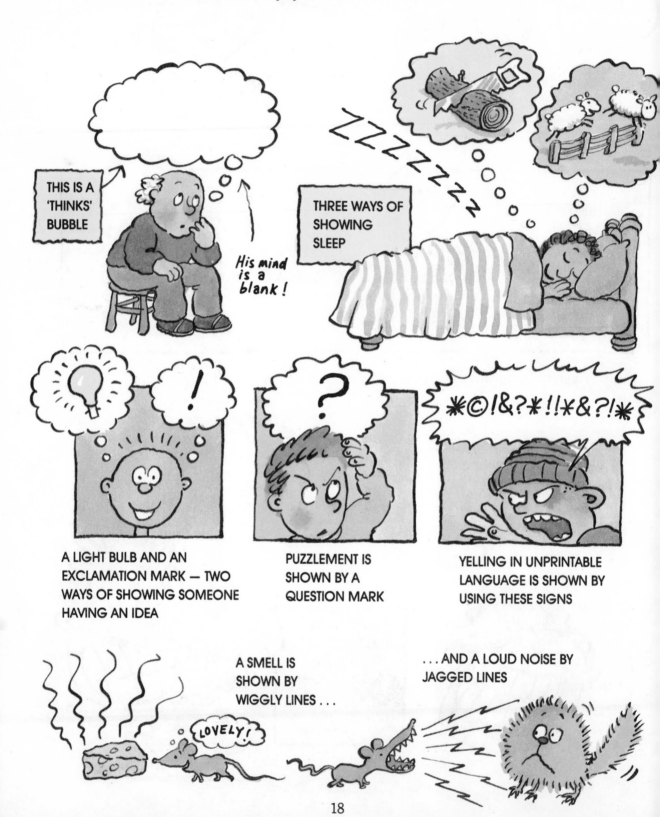

THIS IS A 'THINKS' BUBBLE

His mind is a blank!

THREE WAYS OF SHOWING SLEEP

A LIGHT BULB AND AN EXCLAMATION MARK — TWO WAYS OF SHOWING SOMEONE HAVING AN IDEA

PUZZLEMENT IS SHOWN BY A QUESTION MARK

YELLING IN UNPRINTABLE LANGUAGE IS SHOWN BY USING THESE SIGNS

A SMELL IS SHOWN BY WIGGLY LINES . . .

LOVELY!

. . . AND A LOUD NOISE BY JAGGED LINES

CHARACTERS

Before you attempt a comic strip or cartoon strip of your own it's a good idea to learn how to create your own *characters*. A good cartoon character is a funny drawing of a certain *type* of person (unlike a caricature, which is a funny drawing of an *actual* person – more about that later in the book).

Firstly, try to picture in your mind the character you want to draw. Pick out his or her outstanding features, then *simplify* and *exaggerate*.

For instance, take one of those handsome smoothies that advertise after-shave or read the news on T.V. You know the type . . . square head and chin, thick black eyebrows, small straight nose, mouthful of shiny teeth, slicked-back hair and supercilious grin.

Now, armed with your description, draw the head shape.

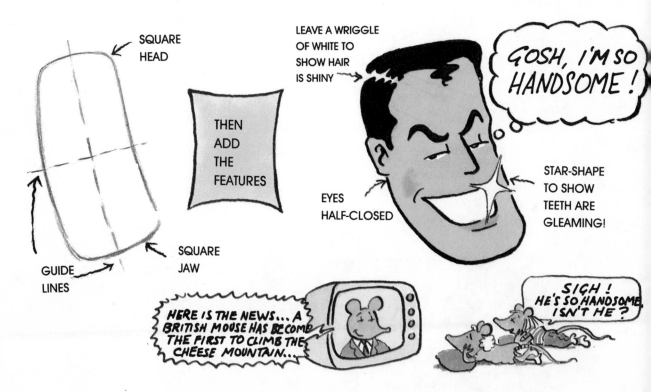

Or how about the winner of a beauty contest?
Small, pointed chin, huge, glossy Dynasty-type hair-do, false eyelashes, big eyes, tiny nose, huge mouth and teeth, curvy figure.

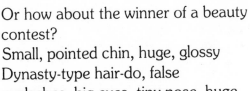

Always start by sketching light guide-lines. For example, to draw a tramp, first sketch in the shape of the body plus the rough outlines of the hat, raincoat and baggy trousers.

THEN ADD THE DETAILS: STUBBLE, PATCHES, HOLES, TOES PEEPING OUT OF SHOES, ETC.

Here's the description of a character I've always liked drawing:
thick black, swept-back hair, sideburns, sunglasses, long (drape) jacket with coloured lapels and flaps, thin legs in tight trousers (drainpipes) and thick-soled, blue-suede shoes. So . . . ready to boogie? Of course! It's a rock 'n roll singer!

Here are some other characters.
I have noted down some of the thoughts I had about each one. Can you
think of more? If you can, try to draw these figures again in your own
way. If you can't, just copy them!

VAMPIRE
EVIL EYES,
POINTED FACE AND TEETH,
BAT CLOAK

SERGEANT-MAJOR
SQUARE JAW, STERN LOOK,
BIG BOOTS

SKATEBOARDER
SAFETY GEAR, PLENTY
OF ACTION

BULLY
SCOWLING FACE,
HUNCHED SHOULDERS, BEEFY
BODY, BIG FISTS

SCIENTIST
THIN FACE
AND BODY, ABSENT-
MINDED LOOK

TENNIS PLAYER
HEAD-BAND, FLYING
HAIR, THIN MUSCLY BODY

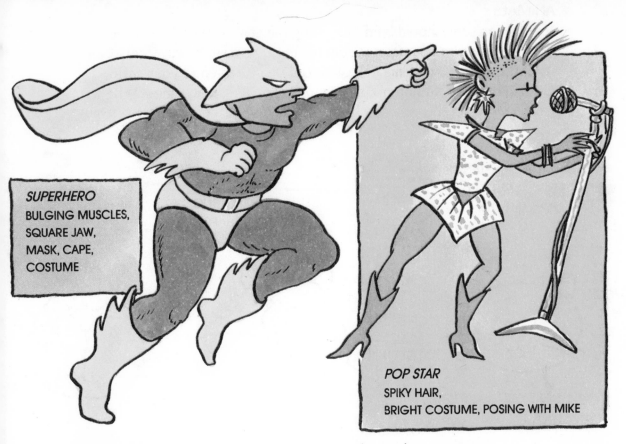

Using the same descriptive technique, you can also make cartoon characters out of objects.

CAR

A TEAPOT

A GUITAR

A TREE

A FLOWER

Use the most obvious features of the object to help you create its 'character': the car's headlamps as eyes, the guitar's sound-hole as mouth, the tree's wrinkly bark as face and branches as hair, etc.

ANIMALS

Animal cartoons should be drawn using the same method you used to draw the cartoon characters. That means you must have a good idea of what the animal looks like in real life before you attempt your cartoon. Cuttings of animal photographs from newspapers, magazines and calendars will come in handy here.

A CAT, FOR INSTANCE, IS EASY. IT USUALLY LOOKS LIKE THIS

SO BY SIMPLIFYING THE SHAPES . . .

YOU GET THIS

EXAGGERATE THE SHAPE SLIGHTLY AND YOU GET THIS

. . . OR THIS!

By using more shapes for the head you get more variation.

HEAD SHAPE

NOSE SHAPE

HEAD SHAPE

CHEEK SHAPES

The main difference between a cat's head and a dog's head is the size of the nose. Cats have small noses . . . dogs have big ones.

LOOK AT THE LENGTH OF THAT DOG'S NOSE! HE MUST HAVE A TERRIFIC SENSE OF SMELL!

NOT REALLY. BY THE TIME THE SMELL GOES FROM HIS NOSE TO HIS BRAIN HE HAS FORGOTTEN WHAT IT WAS!

A BISCUIT? A SOCK? LUNCH?

So to draw an average cartoon dog, exaggerate the nose shape.

But, unlike cats', dogs' heads come in all shapes and sizes.

BLOODHOUND   IRISH SETTER   AFGHAN HOUND   DOBERMANN PINSCHER

And there are hundreds of other breeds!
Your cartoon dog, therefore, can be a funny drawing of an *actual*
dog (almost a caricature, in fact).
Simply exaggerate the outstanding features:

EXAGGERATE THE
BLOODHOUND'S LONG NOSE,
WRINKLES AND SLEEPY LOOK

EXAGGERATE THE
SETTER'S EARS
AND UPTILTED
NOSE

EXAGGERATE THE
AFGHAN'S LONG NOSE
AND LONG HAIR

EXAGGERATE
THE DOBERMANN'S
FIERCE MOUTH
AND MEAN EYES

The shape of the dog's body, of course, will depend on the type of dog you are cartooning.

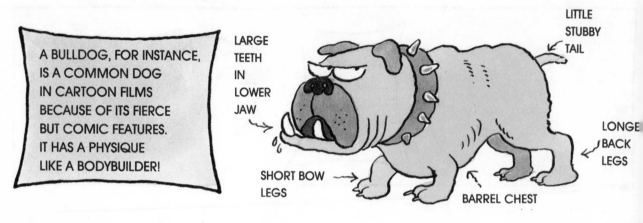

A BULLDOG, FOR INSTANCE, IS A COMMON DOG IN CARTOON FILMS BECAUSE OF ITS FIERCE BUT COMIC FEATURES. IT HAS A PHYSIQUE LIKE A BODYBUILDER!

LARGE TEETH IN LOWER JAW

LITTLE STUBBY TAIL

LONGE BACK LEGS

SHORT BOW LEGS

BARREL CHEST

A cat's body is usually smooth and slinky. So you can make it even more smooth and slinky by exaggerating these points . . .

OR DO THE OPPOSITE TO MAKE IT LOOK FUNNIER!

A lion's body is similar to a cat's, only bigger and more powerful. So start off by thinking about a basic cat shape . . .

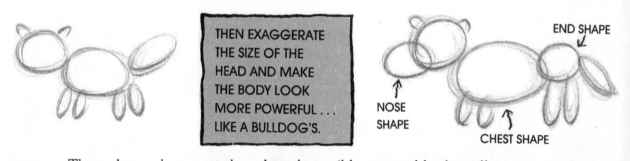

THEN EXAGGERATE THE SIZE OF THE HEAD AND MAKE THE BODY LOOK MORE POWERFUL . . . LIKE A BULLDOG'S.

END SHAPE

NOSE SHAPE

CHEST SHAPE

Then, draw a huge mouth and teeth, a wild mane, add a few effects and . . .

ROAR!

. . . the Lord of the Jungle!

Here are some other animals to try:

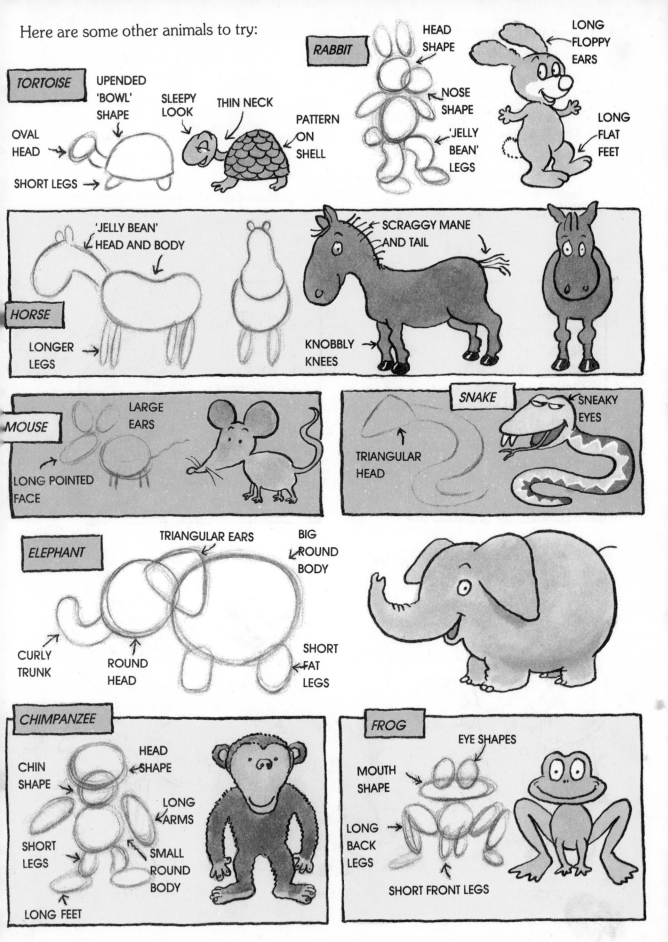

TORTOISE

OVAL HEAD

SHORT LEGS

UPENDED 'BOWL' SHAPE

SLEEPY LOOK

THIN NECK

PATTERN ON SHELL

RABBIT

HEAD SHAPE

LONG FLOPPY EARS

NOSE SHAPE

'JELLY BEAN' LEGS

LONG FLAT FEET

HORSE

'JELLY BEAN' HEAD AND BODY

SCRAGGY MANE AND TAIL

LONGER LEGS

KNOBBLY KNEES

MOUSE

LARGE EARS

LONG POINTED FACE

SNAKE

SNEAKY EYES

TRIANGULAR HEAD

ELEPHANT

TRIANGULAR EARS

BIG ROUND BODY

CURLY TRUNK

ROUND HEAD

SHORT FAT LEGS

CHIMPANZEE

HEAD SHAPE

CHIN SHAPE

LONG ARMS

SHORT LEGS

SMALL ROUND BODY

LONG FEET

FROG

EYE SHAPES

MOUTH SHAPE

LONG BACK LEGS

SHORT FRONT LEGS

ANIMAL CHARACTERS

The animal cartoons on the previous page show you *one* way to draw a particular animal. But, of course, there are lots of ways to do each one. That's what makes cartooning exciting – you can create your very own characters.

For instance, just think of the number of famous cartoon cats there are and how different they all look: Sylvester, Tom, Top Cat, Garfield, etc. Each one has its own strong personality. This is what you must try to achieve. Let's say you want to draw a sly cat character, the kind of feline that would sell its granny for a tin of catfood.

THIS CHARACTER DOESN'T WORK IF HE CAN HELP IT. SO HERE HE IS, LEANING LAZILY AGAINST A LAMP-POST, HAT OVER HIS EYES, ARMS FOLDED, LEGS CROSSED

WHEN YOUR CHARACTER HAS BEEN SKETCHED IN TO YOUR SATISFACTION, FILL IN THE DETAILS: SNEAKY EYES, SLY GRIN, BRIGHT COLOURS, ETC.

Here are some other animal personalities. See if you can supply your own description.

BOXER DOG   *ELEGANT ELEPHANT*   *MARILYN MOUSE*

These animals look funny because they are copying humans. Your own animal cartoon character, therefore, could act like a person – walk on two legs, talk, sleep in a bed and eat with a knife and fork.

YOU ARE TWELVE YEARS OLD AND OUR CARTOON CAT HAS BETTER TABLE MANNERS THAN YOU!

Or you can use your imagination to create cartoon beasts, monsters and dragons.

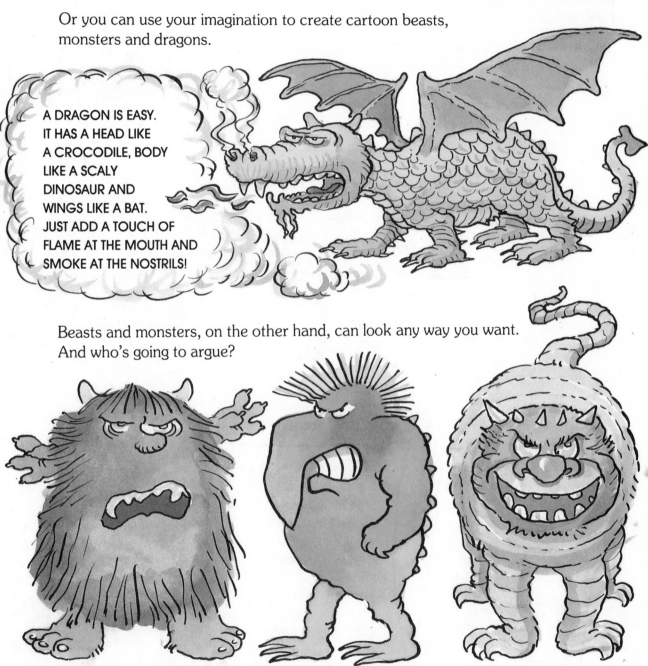

A DRAGON IS EASY. IT HAS A HEAD LIKE A CROCODILE, BODY LIKE A SCALY DINOSAUR AND WINGS LIKE A BAT. JUST ADD A TOUCH OF FLAME AT THE MOUTH AND SMOKE AT THE NOSTRILS!

Beasts and monsters, on the other hand, can look any way you want. And who's going to argue?

USING CARTOONS

Drawing cartoon characters just for the fun of it is great, but it's so much more fun if you *use* your drawings in some way.

FOR INSTANCE, YOU MAY BE ASKED TO DESIGN A POSTER FOR YOUR SCHOOL OR CLUB. SO WHY NOT USE A CARTOON CHARACTER?

USE LIGHT PENCIL GUIDE-LINES FOR YOUR LETTERING

PLACE YOUR FIGURE WHERE YOU WANT IT

THEN INK IN THE OUTLINES, RUB OUT THE GUIDE-LINES WHEN INK IS DRY AND ADD COLOUR

LETTER LIGHTLY WITH A PENCIL FIRST TO MAKE SURE IT FITS!

PARALLEL GUIDE-LINES

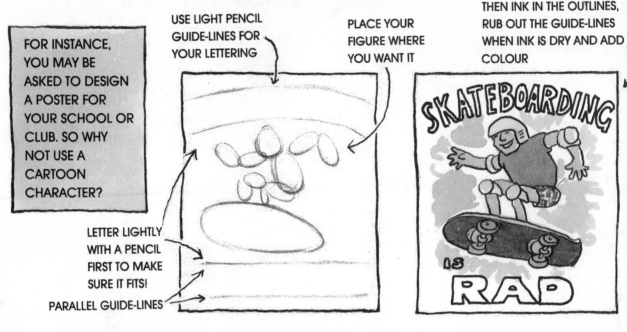

Use cartoon drawings in your letters. For example:

Make your own birthday and Christmas cards.

MAKE YOUR CHRISTMAS CARDS PERSONAL AND SAVE MONEY! DRAW A BLACK-AND-WHITE CARTOON OF, SAY, SANTA IN THE SNOW, GET IT PHOTOCOPIED A FEW TIMES AND STICK THE COPIES ONTO BLANK CARDS.

If you have a good sense of humour then why not try drawing some single-cartoon jokes? (These are usually drawn in black and white.) These must be easy to look at (don't put in too much detail) and must have an obvious joke.

First, think of a character. Second, think of all the situations where this character might do something funny. For instance, let's say your character was a baby.

Try and picture this baby in funny situations. Babies don't do much. They sit around looking cute – so what would happen if it was able to do things you didn't expect?

Here are two examples of this baby in 'impossible' situations. The poor parents are totally mystified!

SHE'S JUST BROKEN THE WORLD RECORD!

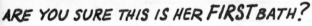

ARE YOU SURE THIS IS HER *FIRST BATH?*

As you can see, the punchline can either be below the drawing or inside it in a speech bubble.

Here are a few fairly common cartoon-joke themes to get your ideas going: MR AND MRS DRACULA, A DESERT ISLAND, PERSON MEETS ALIEN/MONSTER, POSTMAN AND DOG, DOCTOR'S OFFICE, THE BIG BOSS.

BACKGROUNDS

Backgrounds are important not only in single-cartoon jokes but also in cartoon strips because they describe visually where your character is. The main thing to remember here is . . . keep it simple!

You don't want your background to be more important than your character! It is there just to set the scene. For instance, if your character is out of doors then a simple roof-line might be enough to suggest he is in a town.

OR YOU MAY WANT A 'CLOSE-UP' FEELING BY USING A BRICK WALL

IF YOU WANT 'ATMOSPHERE' YOU CAN USE A SIMPLE SOURCE OF LIGHT LIKE A LAMP-POST TO SUGGEST BOTH 'TOWN' AND 'NIGHT'

A greater idea of distance can be achieved by using perspective. Perspective, very simply, is the idea that as objects recede, or go away from you, they look smaller. Here is an example:

ALL OF THESE CITY GENTS ARE THE SAME SIZE BUT THEY SEEM TO GET SMALLER THE FURTHER AWAY THEY ARE

HERE IS THE SAME BACKGROUND AGAIN. NOTICE NOW THE PARALLEL LINES OF THE BUILDING, WINDOWS AND PAVEMENT SEEM TO RUN TOWARDS EACH OTHER AND COME TOGETHER AT VP (THE 'VANISHING' POINT)

HERE IS THE SAME PICTURE AGAIN, ONLY THIS TIME SEEN FROM ABOVE. NOTICE HOW THE VANISHING POINT IS NOW MUCH HIGHER

BUT YOU DON'T NEED TO USE PARALLEL LINES TO SUGGEST PERSPECTIVE. JUST REMEMBER THAT THINGS GET SMALLER AS THEY GET FURTHER AWAY.

TREES GET SMALLER

ROAD GETS NARROWER

FENCE GETS SMALLER

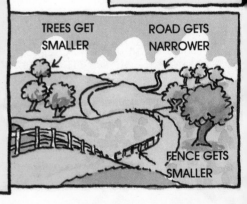

DRAWING AND COLOURING TECHNIQUES

Before you get more ambitious and try to do a strip cartoon (a cartoon joke that uses three or four frames) or even a comic strip (a story in cartoon pictures), it's a good idea to know something about *drawing and colouring techniques*.

What are the best things to use?

The answer to that is . . . different things produce different effects.

COLOUR PENCILS PRODUCE A WARM, SUBTLE EFFECT. IT'S EASY TO BLEND ONE COLOUR WITH ANOTHER.

ANOTHER WAY OF EMPLOYING COLOUR PENCILS IS TO USE 'HATCHING'.
THIS MEANS USING LOTS OF LINES CLOSE TOGETHER FOR SHADING. THIS TYPE OF SHADING CAN MAKE YOUR DRAWING LOOK MORE 'DYNAMIC'.

The hatching technique, however, is best used with a pen (this is what most cartoonists use), either a fibre-tip or a dip pen (the kind you have to dip into ink).

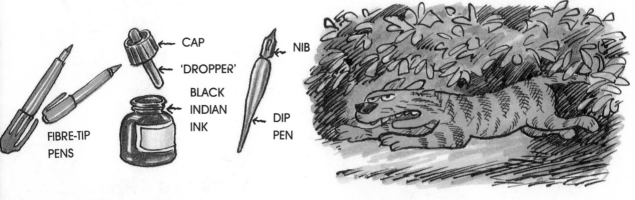

CAP

'DROPPER'

BLACK INDIAN INK

NIB

DIP PEN

FIBRE-TIP PENS

FIBRE-TIP PENS CAN BE USED TO FILL IN SOLID AREAS OF COLOUR AND ALSO TO CREATE PATTERN AND COLOUR BY OVERLAYING LINES.

BLACK OUTLINE

'OVERLAYING' LINES

'SOLID' COLOUR

'SOLID' COLOUR

33

Coloured inks and watercolour are also very good to use as they are bright and vivid. (I've used inks for most of the drawings in this book.)

USE BRUSHES OR DIP PENS WITH INKS

USE BRUSHES WITH WATERCOLOUR

USE DARK COLOURS FOR SHADED AREAS →

IT IS POSSIBLE TO BLEND COLOUR WHILE THEY ARE STILL WET . . . BUT NOT *TOO* WET!

It is advisable to use waterproof ink or black indian ink for your outlines.

YOU DON'T WANT THIS TO HAPPEN WHEN YOU START USING COLOUR

OO-ER! I FEEL ALL FUZZY!

The brightest colours should be used for objects that are nearest to you, paler colours for things that are far away.

I DON'T LIKE THIS PLACE. IT'S TOO CHEERFUL!

A strong source of light and dark shadows can add dramatic atmosphere to your scene.

Another way of producing a dramatic effect is by using silhouettes (solid black shapes).

It is always best to use a softish pencil, say B or 2B, to sketch out your idea. Not only do they give a nicer 'feel' to sketching but also soft pencil lines are easier to erase.

Grades of pencil go from 9B (very soft) to 9H (very hard).

Most pencils bought in ordinary stationer's shops are HB (hard black).

This is an in-between grade of pencil usually used for writing.

CARTOON STRIPS

So how about trying to create your own *cartoon strip*? Like the single cartoon, it's easier to think of a character first then imagine him/her/it in funny situations. And as I said at the beginning of the book, your cartoon character can be anything from a robot to a germ.

Start off by 'doodling' some ideas on scrap paper. Once you have a good idea of the characters and situation you want, transfer your idea to 'good' paper: cartridge paper or artist's board. This is the way professionals work.

Remember, each frame of your strip must not look too cluttered. Keep it simple!

My cartoon-strip idea is about a coloured blob. This is my rough drawing:

THE PRINTING IN THE SPEECH BUBBLES MUST BE CLEAR AND LEGIBLE. DRAW FAINT GUIDE-LINES WITH A RULER AND RUB THEM OUT ONCE YOU HAVE INKED IN THE LETTERING.

REMEMBER TO KEEP YOUR WORK CLEAN!

When you are satisfied with the way it looks 'ink in' over your guide-lines. Here is my finished strip. I inked in the outline with black waterproof ink using a dip pen, then coloured the drawing using inks.

Lettering can be an important ingredient in a cartoon strip. Apart from the printing in speech bubbles you may want to make a feature of a particular word.

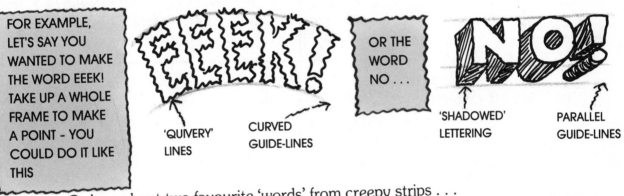

Or how about two favourite 'words' from creepy strips . . .

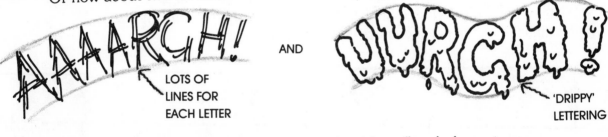

Another way in which lettering is used is in the title or 'logo' of a cartoon strip. See if you can create your own.

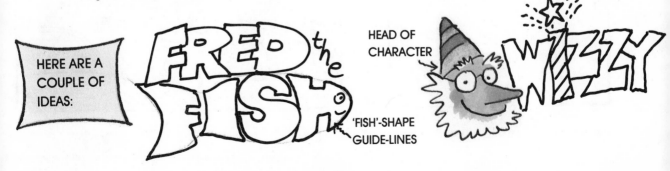

The usual size of a cartoon strip is approximately 5 cm × 18 cm and three to five frames are normally used.

For variety you can leave out the outline of a frame like this:

As long as the dimensions of your strip are roughly those that I mentioned you can do anything.

Comic strips are different. Their size depends on the dimensions and format of the comic in which they appear. But a typical size is around 28 cm × 20 cm.

Also, in a comic strip, different angles and viewpoints are used to stop the pictures becoming repetitive. In fact, comic-strip artists use the same kinds of technique and effect that movie directors use.

'CLOSE-UP'

'LONG-SHOT'

'PANNING' (SHOWING A PANORAMIC VIEW TO SET THE SCENE)

HIGH VIEWPOINTS
(GUIDE-LINES TAPER TOWARDS
BOTTOM OF PICTURE)

LOW VIEWPOINTS
(GUIDE-LINES TAPER TOWARDS
TOP OF PICTURE)

FORESHORTENING

'VOICE-OVER'

COMIC STRIPS

A *comic strip* is a story in pictures, so obviously you have to have a story organized before you start to draw.

DON'T SIT STARING AT A BLANK SHEET OF PAPER WONDERING WHAT TO DRAW

WHAT DO YOU THINK OF MY NEW COMIC STRIP? IT'S CALLED "THE ADVENTURES OF THE INVISIBLE MAN IN A SNOWSTORM."

The best way to go about this is to write a synopsis (shortened version) of your story idea. For instance . . .

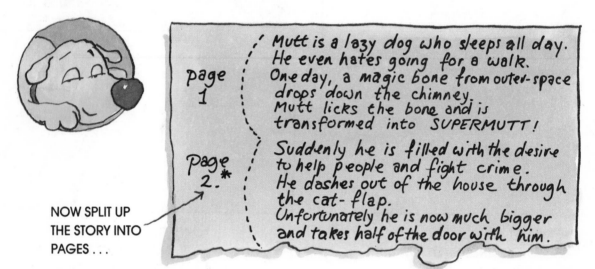

page 1

Mutt is a lazy dog who sleeps all day. He even hates going for a walk. One day, a magic bone from outer-space drops down the chimney. Mutt licks the bone and is transformed into SUPERMUTT!

page 2.*

Suddenly he is filled with the desire to help people and fight crime. He dashes out of the house through the cat-flap. Unfortunately he is now much bigger and takes half of the door with him.

NOW SPLIT UP THE STORY INTO PAGES . . .

Then, work out the story and action for each page.

1st. FRAME. Mutt's owner looks round the door   Asks.. "No walkies today then, Mutt?" Mutt is asleep.

2nd. FRAME. Mutt opens one eye.. thinks.. "Please! I'm trying to rest!"

3rd. FRAME. Close-up of Mutt thinking .. "This is the life.. No ties.. no responsibilities!"

4th. FRAME. An information frame . It says.. "But little did Mutt know that his life was about to be changed FOREVER!"

THIS IS MUCH THE SAME WAY THAT T.V. AND FILM SCRIPT-WRITERS WORK.

. . . etc.

Once you have this information you can 'design' or 'lay out' your page. By this I mean that you can arrange the frames so that the story flows naturally and the 'look' of the page is good and has the greatest impact.

For instance, the frames showing Mutt lying in his basket can be normal size, but the frame showing the bone speeding from Outer Space could be very large to give that image more impact.

Lay out your frame design roughly in pencil like this before you draw the story.

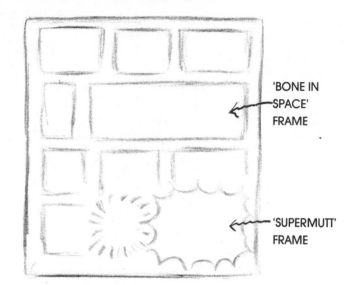

'BONE IN SPACE' FRAME

'SUPERMUTT' FRAME

'THINKS BUBBLES'

INFORMATION IN FRAME TO SET THE SCENE

PART OF DRAWING OUTSIDE FRAME MAKES DESIGN INTERESTING

'DYNAMIC' FRAME SHAPES

CAN YOU CONTINUE THIS STRIP? (USE MY START TO PAGE 2* IF YOU LIKE)

PEOPLE AGAIN

At the beginning of this book I showed you how to draw a simple cartoon face. Now I'll show you how to make that face look any age you choose. Again, draw the basic head shape with guide-lines going through the centre in both directions.

LIKE THIS

TO MAKE THE FACE LOOK YOUNGER, SIMPLY DROP THE EYELINE SLIGHTLY TO LEAVE MORE HEAD SPACE LIKE THIS

ORIGINAL EYELINE

NEW EYELINE

FOR A BABY DROP THE EYELINE EVEN FURTHER BUT MAKE THE HEAD ROUNDER AND THE CHEEKS FATTER

ROUNDER HEAD

ORIGINAL EYELINE

FATTER CHEEKS

NEW EYELINE

CUTE, HUH?

To make the face older, reverse this process. Draw the eyeline slightly higher than normal and make the head thinner.

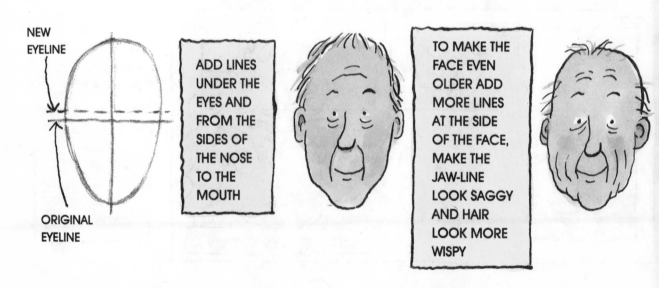

NEW EYELINE

ORIGINAL EYELINE

ADD LINES UNDER THE EYES AND FROM THE SIDES OF THE NOSE TO THE MOUTH

TO MAKE THE FACE EVEN OLDER ADD MORE LINES AT THE SIDE OF THE FACE, MAKE THE JAW-LINE LOOK SAGGY AND HAIR LOOK MORE WISPY

The rules of proportion that apply to real people don't apply to cartoons.

For instance, if you were to draw a real person you would have to be careful of the proportions. The head length usually divides into the body length about seven times.

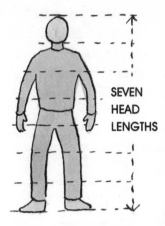

SEVEN HEAD LENGTHS

IF YOU MAKE THE HEAD TOO BIG, THEN YOUR PERSON MAY START TO LOOK LIKE A CARTOON CHARACTER. SO . . .!

The general rule of proportion for cartoon characters is . . . make the head *large* in comparison to the body.

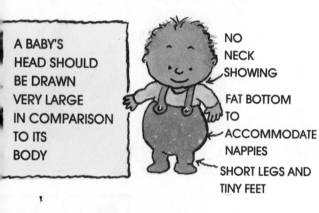

A BABY'S HEAD SHOULD BE DRAWN VERY LARGE IN COMPARISON TO ITS BODY

NO NECK SHOWING

FAT BOTTOM TO ACCOMMODATE NAPPIES

SHORT LEGS AND TINY FEET

AN OLD PERSON'S SHAPE MAY BE MORE ROUNDED, THE HEAD DIVIDING INTO THE BODY LENGTH ABOUT FOUR TIMES

FOUR HEAD LENGTHS

OR THEN AGAIN THE OLD PERSON COULD BE TALL AND THIN AND ANGULAR . . . BUT STILL THE HEAD WOULD FIT INTO THE BODY LENGTH ONLY ABOUT FIVE TIMES

FIVE HEAD LENGTHS

These are general rules to follow when drawing cartoons. But, of course, your cartoon character's shape can be as exaggerated as you like!

CARICATURES

Caricatures are funny drawings of actual people and are probably the hardest type of cartoon to do as they have to be recognizable! However, if you describe the person to yourself as you did when you were drawing the cartoon characters (remember the news-reader and the beauty queen?) then this will help you get a likeness.

Also, the cartooning rules of *simplify* and *exaggerate* still apply.

RIGHT, HERE WE GO . . .

THERE ARE 3 IMPORTANT POINTS TO LOOK FOR . . .

1 HEAD SHAPE COULD IT BE ONE OF THESE?

WEDGE BALL PEANUT PEAR

EGG BLOCK JELLY-BEAN OVAL TRIANGULAR

2 OUTSTANDING FEATURES

UPTURNED NOSE STARING EYES CURLY MOUTH BIG EARS

3 FACIAL EXPRESSION

SLEEPY BRIGHT JOLLY MOROSE

The variations, of course, are endless. What you have to do is *study* the face you are drawing and make sure you know what these three points are.

Now who should you caricature? Pals, parents, relatives, teachers . . . anyone, in fact!

But before you do, get some practice by doing caricatures of people in newspaper and magazine photographs. I picked out a few at random and caricatured them to give you an idea of the process.

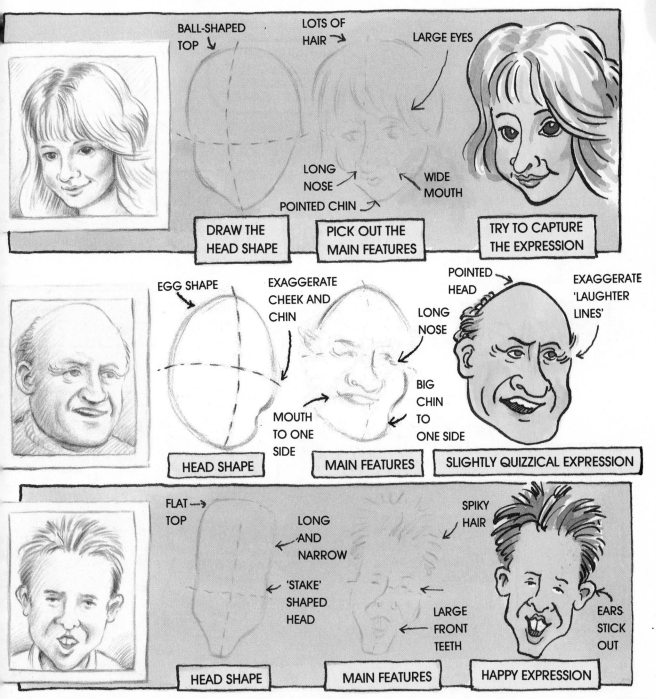

BALL-SHAPED TOP ↓

LOTS OF HAIR →

LARGE EYES

LONG NOSE

WIDE MOUTH

POINTED CHIN ↗

DRAW THE HEAD SHAPE

PICK OUT THE MAIN FEATURES

TRY TO CAPTURE THE EXPRESSION

EGG SHAPE

EXAGGERATE CHEEK AND CHIN

POINTED HEAD

EXAGGERATE 'LAUGHTER LINES'

LONG NOSE

BIG CHIN TO ONE SIDE

MOUTH TO ONE SIDE

HEAD SHAPE

MAIN FEATURES

SLIGHTLY QUIZZICAL EXPRESSION

FLAT → TOP

LONG AND NARROW

SPIKY HAIR

'STAKE' SHAPED HEAD

LARGE FRONT TEETH

EARS STICK OUT

HEAD SHAPE

MAIN FEATURES

HAPPY EXPRESSION

If you enjoy drawing cartoons and would like to get better at it then here are a few tips to keep in mind.

1. Practise as much as you can.

2. Read all you can about cartoonists, and how they work (as well as reading this book, of course!).

3. Look at cartoonists' work in comics, newspapers and magazines and copy it.

4. Keep a sketchbook and use it every day. Don't worry about what to put in it; just draw . . . objects, people, animals . . . anything that interests you.

Finally, here is a re-run of the most important points from this book.